# GOD'S FAVOR 4 TEEN GIRLS

**By Phyllis Haugabook**

Copyright © 2009 by Phyllis Haugabook

*God's Favor 4 Teen Girls*
by Phyllis Haugabook

Printed in the United States of America

ISBN 978-1-60791-555-3

All rights reserved solely by the author. The author guarantees all contents are original and do not infringe upon the legal rights of any other person or work. No part of this book may be reproduced in any form without the permission of the author. The views expressed in this book are not necessarily those of the publisher.

Unless otherwise indicated, Bible quotations are taken from The New Open Bible Study Edition: The New King James Version of the Bible. Copyright © 1972 by Thomas Nelson, publisher.

www.xulonpress.com

# Table Of Contents

Dedication ............................................................. vii

Introduction .......................................................... ix

#1
It's a Girl Thang........13

#2
Sister, Girl, What is Up with the Love that You
Do Not Have for Yourself?........23

#3
The Depths of my Soul..........33

#4
I'm the Head, not the Tail. Above
and Not Beneath..........41

#5
You Cannot Rely on What's
in Your Head..........51

**#6**
**What Do I Do Once I have Gotten Off My Knees?**.........**59**

**#7**
**Out of the Ashes, into His Hands**........**67**

**#8**
**There's No God Like Jehovah.**.........**77**

# Dedication

This journal is dedicated to my deceased mother, Essie Lee Haugabook, who once was who became
> A girl,
> A woman,
> A mother,
> A Big Momma and
> A Great Big Momma.

***Momma, this is your Amen.***

This journal is also dedicated to all of my nieces, who are inspiring young woman.

## Introduction
# God's Favor 4 Teen Girls

Have you ever thought about why God CREATED girls?

I believe that he created girls because we are designed to serve him with all of our hearts, souls, and minds. In Psalms 139, which is one of favorite passages, it talks about us being fearfully and wonderfully made, that we are made marvelous by him who created us. You may have wondered throughout your life, "Why did God create me this way? Why do I have the eyes that I do? The lips? This nose? This hair? These teeth? These hips, and legs, and last but not least, these feet?"

I'm glad that you're asking these questions, because God needs every inch of you to serve him. Each person is created in his image and his likeness, but do you believe that you're fearfully and wonderfully made by his marvelous hands?

The purpose of this journal is simple: It came directly from a commandment that God spoke into my life, for me to write about the struggles that young women have, and encourage them with the inspirational words of Jesus Christ. I believe that most girls are completely unaware of how beautiful they are. Most girls look at themselves in the mirror and say to themselves, "Oh, I'm too ugly," or "I'm too fat," or "My body is not complete," or "There's something missing from my life."

No matter what you may think about yourself, God knew exactly what he was doing when he created you in his image. When he created you, he knew your faults, your shortcomings, and how you would eventually feel about yourself, your body, and your self-image. When you look at yourself in the mirror, if you do not see the beauty of who you are looking back at you, then you've misunderstood the Gospel.

Not only have you misunderstood the Gospel, but you deny yourself and others the pleasure of loving you for who you are, because you must know that God made no mistakes when he created you in his image.

We live in a culture saturated with lies coming from the media. Television, movies, and magazines give us this false message that as women, we must look like the models on the cover of fashion and glamour magazines. Let me tell you a secret: the models on those magazine covers don't really look like their photos. Beauty is truly in the eye of the beholder.

If you're a young woman and you've struggled with these lies that have caused you confusion about your body image and how you feel about yourself, the wait is now over. It is time for you to get out from underneath this bus and get back in the driver's seat.

After you read this inspirational journal, I would be very surprised if your thoughts didn't completely change about how you feel about yourself. As a women myself, I have struggled with self-esteem and body image, and was convinced at one point in my life that I was worthless.

But now I'm fully convinced that I'm fearfully and wonderfully made by the marvelous hands of God, who created me in his image. No matter how you feel about yourself, God isn't through with you yet. My prayer is that now after reading this introduction, you have a hunger to continue to read, pray and meditate with the help of the Holy Spirit and this journal. I also pray that your life would be changed from the inside out.

Well, the time is now. Let's get started on this journey together.

# #1

# It's a Girl Thang

I'm writing this journal entry after I spent the day with some of the most fabulous women of God. When I spent time with them, I sensed that these women were filled with the Holy Spirit, simply by loving on our Lord and Savior through praise and worship. Before I decided to leave my house and spend time with them, I was having second thoughts about staying home. I considered not going because I was in a very dry spot, spiritually, and I just wanted to live in my dryness, and not leave my home. Before I left my house, I had to battle with the negative voices in my head trying to tell me to stay home with my spiritually dry self, and continue being in this spot spiritually.

It was so easy for me to sit at home, wrapped in my quilt, staring at the four walls with a blank look on my face, and make an attempt to watch my favorite TV shows, like ***Gunsmoke, CNN,*** and ***CSI.*** On that day, I didn't want to be bothered with fellowship or see anyone. Six months prior to this, my mother had passed away. Honestly, I didn't want to be anywhere but to sit on my couch in my sorrow and despair.

This women's fellowship was the last place I wanted to be. Not because I knew that I wouldn't be blessed, but because it would take so much of an effort to use my emotional, physical, and spiritual energy. On that day, thinking about the emotional, physical, and spiritual effort that it would take to leave my house made me feel nauseated. I would have to spend time with people, and on that day I wasn't in the mood. My attitude that day was that it was "OK" for me to worship my sorrow and despair instead of worshiping God.

Now, do not get me wrong. I love being with God and worshiping him, but on that day, my attitude was, "Are you kidding me? Don't you people understand just how much my sorrow and despair have taken over my life?"

I had to physically force myself to get up off the couch. As I got to my feet, I said to myself and to the temptation to give up and stay home, "Not today. I'm off this couch because I'm going to be spiritually fed with the word of God." As a result of taking this stance, when I arrived at the home fellowship there was an air of excitement. Everyone who was there had this anticipation to worship the Lord Jesus Christ. Our sole purpose of gathering together on that day was to worship the Lord.

As we sang praises, clapped our hands, stomped our feet, got up off of the couch, and started singing like it was our last breath, it made me realize that as women, our spiritual battle really belongs to the Lord.

As women, we have a tremendous battle on our hands. Especially when it comes to managing our spiritual lives. We need each other more than we think. As women, some of us suffer in silence. It is not meant for any of God's people to suffer in silence. Most women are painfully isolated because they've been hurt by other women who they once called their closest girl friends. These same women are isolated and too fearful to reach out to a sister in Christ for help, because she wants to avoid feeling the flood of her own pain.

When I attend church, I've noticed that if a sister shows up to church dressed to kill, with her hair flipped and bouncing, her nails sparkling, and she is dressed in her finest apparel, this doesn't mean that she is emotionally and spiritually intact. Please do not assume that your friend who is sitting next to you on a Sunday morning, smiling, singing, and praising God with all her heart and soul, that her life and soul are intact.

I have discovered that when we come to church, we put on this pseudo-self that says life is just peachy. We try to convince others that our lives are peachy. Many Christian women are angry, isolated, and confused about their roles as wives and mothers. In addition to feeling isolated and confused, they feel hopeless, helpless, and filled with despair, because so few of us are available for the hurting women in our congregations. We serve a holy God filled with forgiveness, mercy and grace, just waiting for us to fall into his arms.

## ONE DAY, WE ALL MAY GET IT RIGHT

I have taken a stance, and I'm praying and asking you to take the same stance, and that is to not listen to another lie, another piece of gossip about another sister as long as you live. Taking this position COULD cause you to lose friends. To not gossip isn't popular with us, because we want to hear the gory details of another person's life. Making this decision may result in losing some close friends, or if you take this stance, you may gain some new friends.

The reason for taking this stance is because we have a spiritual war, and this war impacts the lives of God's people more than we think. People need the saving grace of Jesus Christ, because people are dying every day and their lives may not have been impacted by the saving grace of Jesus Christ. As a young woman, you're going to have moments in your life where you're going to feel spiritually dry. It is in these moments that I guarantee you are going to have personal periods of vulnerabilities and frustrations. When this does happen, do not become fearful of the next steps that the Lord is taking you through. Just remember that this journey isn't for any Lone Rangers.

1 Peter 4:17: "For time has come for judgment to begin at the house of God, and if it

begins with us first, what will be the end of those who do not obey the gospel of God?"

If the righteous one is scarcely saved, where would the ungodly and the sinner appear? (Food for thought.)

I really enjoy reading the above scripture because it is so very clear about the righteous suffering, and if we aren't right with our own relationship with the Lord, then how much of a witness can we be to the world around us?

**Notes:**

**Notes:**

## Questions for #1:

*Where do you stand with your close friends?*

*Do you need to ask forgiveness, or do you need to forgive yourself?*

**Notes:**

#2

# Sister, Girl, What is Up with the Love that You Do Not Have for Yourself?

When you look at yourself in the mirror, if you do not see the face of God looking back at you, saying that you're "fearfully and wonderfully made," then you have misunderstood the message of the Gospel.

Too many times, we look to other people to get our validation. There are times when we do need others to validate us, but do not let that be the reason you get up in the morning. When you get up in the morning thinking negative things about yourself, then your road map for that day will result in negativity *unless* you take the drive down a victorious street.

Maybe one day you did get out of bed, went to school, and something "bad" happened, and you said to yourself, "WHY did I not just stay in bed with the covers over my head?" I HAVE said the same to myself, especially after I have gotten to work and something went wrong, or if someone said something to me that I took the wrong way.

What does this have to do with loving yourself? It has everything to do with it. For, women and young ladies, we often feel guilty if we do not please everyone around us. The saying goes, "If I cannot please everyone in my immediate life (family or friends), then there must be something wrong with me."

Did God create you to please everyone in your life?

NO. He created you to worship him in spirit and in truth, because he inhabits the praises of his people. If you're born again, then you understand that loving God is loving the new creation that he created you to be. As ambassadors for Christ, we are set aside to be a new person in him. The old person that you were once before is no longer there. However, we need to be aware that the lies of the enemy are endless. Satan will try to make you believe that you're worthless, insignificant, and that God has abandoned you. Satan will try to bring up your past, and everything you did wrong.

Are we going to do everything right in our lives?

NO. No one does everything right in their lives. As a young girl, you're going to make mistakes and have hard days. When your day starts, you might not want to get out of bed, go to school, complete your chores, go to church, or listen to your parents. Prayerfully, hang in there. Better days are ahead for you.

One of the things that I have discovered throughout my life is that my love for myself doesn't rely on how "good" or "bad" the day has gone for me. It is all based on my relationship with Jesus Christ, my intercessor, who sits at the right hand of God.

Imagine, as he sits at the right hand of God, he is simultaneously pushing back the gates of hell, and protecting us from the evil one. There is absolutely nothing that can separate me from the love of Jesus Christ. Read Romans chapter 8, verses 34-35. "Who is he who condemns? It is Christ who died and furthermore is also risen, who is even at the right hand of God who also makes intercession for us." v 35: "Who shall separate us from the love of Christ? Shall tribulation or distress, or persecution, or famine, or nakedness, or peril or sword?"

> Ephesians 6:12: "For we do not wrestle against flesh and blood, but against principalities, against powers, against the rulers of the darkness of this age, against spiritual hosts of wickedness in the heavenly places."

As women, the biggest fight we have is battling low self-esteem: lack of self-confidence, poor self-image, comparing ourselves to others, and believing the lies of the enemy. These things, and many more in the realm of the spirit that we have to fight, go beyond the scope of this journal. No girl should be compared to other girls. As adults and parents, we secretly compare our children to one another, not meaning to hurt them, but because we want them to have a great life.

Another reason parents secretly compare their children to other children is because they believe that their children have the capability to blossom into great people with the right instruction. If these girls truly knew just how special they were to their parents, these same girls would jump through hoops to please their parents. I believe that most parents and adults who take care of children want the best for them, because these adults know that greatness is created and not made.

An example of this is that your parents might have tried to expose you to different events, clubs, and organizations, so that you can get excited about the possibility of discovering something new about yourself. Let's just say for fun that your parents signed you up for a science club, and felt that by attending this club you would develop friends and maybe get interested in the sciences. After going to this club for a while you began to think to yourself, "Hey I could become the next girl who could win the Nobel Peace Prize." There are endless possibilities of becoming the next great person.

If you're a parent reading this journal, you may unintentionally compare your children, and are unaware of how they feel about being compared. Comparison could either help or hurt, it all depends on how the comparison is being delivered and received. To love ourselves through the eyes of others is not a bad thing, but we need to get out of the way, and let God work on the inside of us and show us his true, authentic love.

As a young lady, you need to be loved in a way that is concrete, because as you grow from girlhood into womanhood, you're going to need love from others that confirms your womanhood. At this time in your life, you might have a crush on a boy in your class, and you may want confirmation that he loves you, but if he doesn't return that love, your heart is broken.

As a woman, I understand how it feels to have a broken heart. It can make you very "crazy." However, as you grow as a Godly woman, you will learn that people will fail you, and you will fail them. Remember this: as we fail, God continues to have positive thoughts toward us with an expected future, outcome, and a hope for us. Read Jeremiah 29:11. "For I know the thoughts that I think toward you, says the Lord, thoughts of peace and not of evil to give you a future and a hope."

So, Sister, Girl, the next time you get out of bed, and you're feeling low, do kick your feet up, and walk proudly with your head held high, because you belong to the KING of KINGS!!!!

> Isaiah 43:1-3: "I have called you by your name, you're mine. When you pass through the waters I will be with you. And through the rivers, they shall not overflow you. When you walk through the fire, you shall not be burned. Nor shall the flame scorch you. For

I am your Lord your God. The Holy One of Israel, your Savior. I gave Egypt for your ransom."

**Notes:**

**Notes:**

## Questions for #2:

*This is also a good entry for parents.*

*When was the last time you did a love check-up on your life?*

*What do you need to say to yourself to get in alignment with Jesus Christ?*

**Notes:**

#3

# The Depths of my Soul.

Over the past 20 years, I have had the absolute pleasure of counseling many young women. These young women whom I have counseled come from various economic levels, different races, different ages, and each of them, in their own way, has said, "I feel worthless, misunderstood, mistreated, abandoned, abused, and just simply misused by people in my life." They've expressed their intimate feelings of anger, feeling unwanted, and not understood by the adults in their lives.

It really hurts God's heart when young women are very definite that their situation isn't going to change. I can tell you from my own experience on this day that God knows about your situation, and he loves you just the same. Jesus' death on the cross was for every young woman to have the abundant life, and have it to the full. When you're feeling unwanted, and have thoughts racing in your head about how awful you feel about yourself, believing that no one loves you, then let me challenge you to take a long, hard look at why your thoughts aren't matching up with what God created you to be. Some of the girls who I've counseled have expressed their feelings of being unwanted and unloved because they experienced some form of abuse in their lives. No matter what nature of any abuse you may experienced, or someone you know may have experienced, it is all wrong. To have these burdens on one's back, and to try to make sense of them, is overwhelming for any person. So, where does God stand on abuse?

He HATES IT. God DOESN'T agree with any form of abuse, because it isn't in his character to do so. He definitely doesn't agree with the negativity that we fill our minds with about ourselves. It is not in God's plan for any woman to be mistreated, or for her needs to go unmet. If you were abused, abandoned, mistreated, misunderstood, and as a result you feel like a worthless human being, these feelings come from a wounded heart.

The question to ask yourself is: "Why is my heart wounded?" To get to the root of a wounded heart, we must be able to clearly identify the cause. Most people flounder around wounded in life, because they refuse to take a long, hard look at the root cause of their pain. When that happens, their pain becomes infectious. Their infectious pain, their hurt and destruction, bleeds onto other people, ESPECIALLY those close to them.

In other words: HURTING PEOPLE HURT OTHER PEOPLE.

The reality is that most of us know people in our culture, families, churches, communities, school, and work, who have some form of an unresolved issue or issues in their lives. The question then is, "What is a woman to do?"

First, do not feel that you're responsible for another person's pain, especially if you weren't the direct cause of it. Yes, most of us have hurt other people, but not intending to. Sometimes we say or do things that we later regret.

Be careful in how you communicate with a person who is hurting, because sometimes a hurting person's perspective isn't always clear. If you're trying to resolve a hurt from the past, try to communicate with this person when you both have clear heads. If you're not sure about trying to reconnect with a hurting person in your life, always pray about it or talk it over with someone who has Godly wisdom and trustworthy character.

> Isaiah 43:2-3 is one of my favorite scriptures. I hope that it becomes one of your favorite scriptures: "When you pass through the waters, I will be with you. And through the rivers they shall not overflow you. When you walk through the fire you shall not be burned. Nor shall the flame scorch you. For I am the Lord your God, the Holy One of Israel. I gave Egypt for your ransom."

Remember, God wants us to be completely whole. To do his work, he has called each of us to do something special with him. For you to know what he has called you to do, you have to spend time with him. You have to spend time listening to his direction and waiting for an answer to move ahead in the direction he is calling you.

One thing that he is calling each of us to do is simply to be partners with Jesus Christ to reach the world with his love. Your world could be your neighborhood, your church, your park, or simply your classroom.

Just remember: No matter where your world is, God is traveling the road with you.

**Notes:**

**Notes:**

## Questions for #3:

*Why is my heart wounded?*

*What do I do now?*

**Notes:**

# #4

# I'm the Head, not the Tail. Above and Not Beneath.

The title for this entry was inspired by one of my favorite songs (The Blessing of Abraham).

As you serve Jesus Christ as your Lord, and Savior, you're going to be faced with a lot of people who may or may not understand why you're standing for Christ. Your friends, and maybe even your parents, may not understand the call that God has placed on your life.

Even if they do not understand "the call" that God has placed on your life, you cannot give up or give in to their lack of understanding. If you give up or give in on what God has called you to do, you will miss out on something fantastic for your life. I wouldn't be surprised if God is trying to give you a message to separate from certain people, so he could take your life on a different path. God could be talking to you about saying goodbye to certain people in your life, or people who may bring you down. Saying goodbye or "No" to a friend isn't easy.

I started college with several "best friends forever" from my high school in San Francisco, but everyone else dropped out the first year of college. That was a very lonely and difficult time for me, but I knew there was no turning back for me. I had to go on.

Another thing that I had to face up to was the fact that I knew very few people who had careers and college degrees. Even though I didn't know anyone personally with a college degree, I knew that I had to press forward. I knew deep down inside that I had to make hard decisions for my life. Even though others didn't see the vision that God had placed in my life, I still needed to follow the path he had set for me. Making a decision to go to college was an exciting time in my life. It really opened up doors for me that catapulted my career as a therapist.

Believe me, whatever God is leading you to do, if it is his plan for your life, he will open the door for it to happen. God has a plan for your existence, and he will somehow, through his supernatural powers, bring it all together behind the scenes of our lives.

When God is working on our behalf behind the scenes, we're not going to know all the intricate details that he has planned for us. This is where trust comes in. Trusting and waiting on God is the cornerstone for our lives. While you're waiting on God to open a door and to tell you which direction to go down, if you do not hear what you would like to hear, do not give in to your own ideas. Sometimes God doesn't answer us the way we want him to answer us. Waiting on God can be very long and tiresome. While you're waiting for an answer from God, continue to live your life. Do not get discouraged, because that is an open door for the enemy to use our discouragement to his advantage.

More importantly, there could possibly be things in your life that the Lord needs to address before you take your plunge. Think about the areas of your life where you know he is speaking to you. Take a long, hard look at these areas, and ask yourself:

"What is God telling me?"
"What is he trying to teach me?"
"Have I been listening to me?"
"Have I shut God out of my life because I haven't heard what I want to hear from him?"

What are you ready for in your life?

Are you really ready to take the path that God has planned for your life, to subsequently listen to God, shut people out from your life, and hear the message of the cross?

To shut people out from our lives and quiet ourselves before God isn't always an easy thing to do, because as soon as we begin this process, sometimes distractions get even louder.

An example of this could be your "best friends forever" demand to spend more time with you. You would rather spend more time with them, but this could sometimes be problematic. It is great to have friends who care about us and who want to spend time with us as we go through our vision with God. However you may have to say, "NO" to your friends when they want to hang out at your house and talk on the phone to their boyfriends and spend all nighters in your home. When this happens, you want to have fun with your friends and maybe put off spending time with God. It isn't easy leaving them and trying to quiet yourself before God and to hear his message. Believe me, no one wants to be considered a wallflower, or be seen as the girl who takes her Christianity too seriously.

However, there's nothing wrong with taking your Christianity seriously. It is important to you and it is important to God. As woman, not only do we have to balance our lives for our friends to spend time with us, we have to balance our lives to spend time with our families, and time with God.

Have your parents ever wondered and asked you, "Why is this person your friend?" Your answer to them is, "Because there's something about them that makes me feel alive." When you hear their voice, their name, or listen to someone else talk about them, you smile, and your eyes get bigger, which makes you come to attention. In addition to your exhilaration when you see this person, your stomach ties in knots or it is filled with endless butterflies. At the same time, you want so badly to laugh out loud, because you feel completely silly and elated with excitement. More importantly, when you're not around this individual, you're sad, hopeless, and filled with despair. During this desperate mood, you might say to yourself "If I could only touch them, see them, or smell their fragrance, I will be okay."

Hey we're on to something, because when you work in partnership with Jesus Christ, he wants for you to feel the same way about him that you feel about your friends. God wants us as his friends and in his presence, so that he can speak to us about our future.

If any people have ever spoken either positive or negative words about your life, their words could possibly impact who you become. However, God wants to impact who we are today. Having grown up in church, I have heard people say, "I will come to Jesus Christ after I've cleaned myself up." No amount of cleaning yourself up is going to help you come to the Lord. He wants you just as you are. When you experience fear, you might say to yourself, "What could I possibly do for the Kingdom of God?" Well, my dear, God has plenty for you to do.

Coming to the Lord and learning more about who you are in him isn't a dress rehearsal.

There's no time to get dressed up for your life, because it will hit you hard when you least expect it. However, when your life hits you hard, God is still there, waiting for you to come and join him just as you are.

So what are you waiting for? Let's get started!

*This entry was also inspired by five young women in my life, whom I have known all of their lives: my nieces. They've inspired me because they've had tremendous obstacles in their lives, and now they're raising some of the most inspiring children, my great-nieces and nephews. You go, girls!!!!*

Jeremiah chapter 29:11 is a purposeful scripture for this time: "For I know the thoughts that I think toward you, says the Lord, thoughts of peace and not of evil, to give you a future and a hope."

This entry was also inspired by Proverbs 3:5-6 and Deuteronomy 28:13, which are very encouraging scriptures as you travel the road with God.

Proverbs 3: 5-6: "Trust in the Lord with all your heart, and lean not on your own understanding; In all your ways acknowledge him, and he shall direct your paths."

Deuteronomy 28:13: "And the Lord will make you the head and not the tail; You shall be above only, and not be beneath, if you heed the commandments of your Lord your God, which I command you today, and are careful to observe them."

**Notes:**

**Notes:**

## Questions for #4:

*So, who says that you're not the Head, that you're a Tail, not Above, and not Beneath?*

*What do you say back to them in defense of who you are in Christ?*

*What do you need to do to get the junk out of your life, to get closer to God?*

**Notes:**

#5

# You Cannot Rely on What's in Your Head.

When you start your day, have you ever found your mind wandering, preoccupied with negative thinking? As a result of this, these same negative thoughts try to sit with you while you eat your breakfast. These same negative thoughts try to hang on, and try to follow you to school. They continuously try to pound your mind with negative thinking, behaviors, and actions.

Even as you come home toward the end of the day, tired, with a lot on your plate, these same negative thoughts are still trying to hang on and impact your life. Consequently, as you lay your head down at night, these same intrusive, negative thoughts start all over again. As you move through your life, no matter how hard you pray, these same thoughts continue to stay in your head. When you try to get rid of these thoughts, you might feel like taking your fist to pound sense into your head. Is it that easy, to simply lie down, knock sense into our heads, and rid our minds of these fleshly thoughts that travel throughout our minds?

Like you, I, too, have lain awake late at night, pondering certain things that I knew God was taking care of, but for some reason I couldn't let go of the constant worry about these unresolved issues in my life.

The flesh of my mind wasn't going to cooperate with God's word. Do not get me wrong, I read his word, mediate on his word, pour his word over my life, attend church, attend Bible study, prayer meetings etc. Throughout all of this prostrating before God, I BEGAN to realize that I was doing all of the right things, but what it takes to succeed is for me (Phyllis) to solely depend of God.

I have to every day hand my life over to him, because everything he says in his word is a pillar for my life. On the other hand, our flesh doesn't want to let go of the old way of thinking. It wants to hang on like "ugly on an ape." This is a quote from **Gunsmoke.** Anyway, back to scripture.

> In Romans 12:2, it reads: "And do not conform to this World but be ye transformed by the renewing of your mind, that you may prove what is that good and acceptable, and Perfect will of God."

As women, we have to face up to the fact that there are tremendous challenges we face in the 21st

Century. As a young woman, when you begin the developmental, spiritual, and emotional process of crossing over from girlhood into womanhood, you will face drastic changes in your life. These changes include your mind, your thoughts, your emotions, your spiritual life, your body, your relationships, and your finances. As a woman, I have learned that the transformation from girlhood into womanhood is an evolution, not a dress rehearsal.

As a young woman, you've modeled your life from women in your family, and in your community you've watched them cultivate their lives with tremendous success and pain.

However, as you grow up, you've spent countless hours watching your mother and other women cook, clean, take care of you, take care of your brothers and sisters, and your father, and you've also watched them take care of other people's children. As we watch our mothers and these other women with these dubious duties, we secretly and openly say to ourselves, "This will never be my life." How often do we say this, and we somehow end up eating these words?

There were many things that I ADMIRED about my mother. The one thing that sticks out in my experiences as her daughter is how she lived a very simple life.

It was some time after my mother's death that I realized the symbolism of how simple her life was. My mother grew up living with parents whose lives were very simple. Their motto was "You take and use whatever God has placed in your hands, and you use these gifts until God repositions you to a different level in life."

Now, at this time in my life, I want my life to be simple in its simplicity. It helps me to realize even more that it doesn't matter what I have in my life, because it all belongs to God.

I remember growing up, thinking for many years that I had to get myself out of this simple mindset, and do something big and important. And here I am today, wanting more and more each day a simple lifestyle. In other words, you cannot trust every word that floats around in your mind. I believe that God may be directing you to do certain things, like leaving an area or maybe starting a new relationship, or even renewing an old friendship, or he could be challenging you to take a long hard look at the type of men you've been dating, who aren't for your best interest.

Knowing God the way that I do, he is probably trying to open and close certain doors in your life. God makes many efforts to get our attention. He desires our attention, so that he can speak to us about our lives. I challenge you to listen to the quiet voice from the Holy Spirit that is speaking to you about these areas. We have an ever-changing spiritual war zone in our minds, and these thoughts try to convince us that we know what is best for our lives.

**Notes:**

**Notes:**

## Questions for #5:

My question to you today: *What is happening in your life at this moment that's the source of too much complexity, and not enough simplicity in your life?*




As much as we plan to live our lives a certain way, there are events, people, and just plain ordinary life that comes in and grabs hold of us like a tidal wave or an undertow. I pray that you take some time with God today and make a list of things that you could do to simplify your life.

*What can I do today?*

**Notes:**

#6

# What Do I Do Once I have Gotten Off My Knees?

Usually when you're on a supernatural high, the enemy of your soul tries everything in his power to bring you down from this high. He doesn't care who you are, or what you've done and will do for the Kingdom of God. He certainly does not care that this journal would have an impact on the lives of many young women in our communities. When I began this process of writing and creating this journal, there were times when I thought, "Who's going to read this journal?" I had negative conversations in my mind, back and forth, about writing this journal, with the distorted belief that no one would read them.

More importantly, I have been pleasantly surprise by the positive feedback that I have received from friends, family members, and my colleagues about the substance of these newsletters.

I can honestly tell you that I've spent a number of years, journaling my heart out, trying to discover how to put my mess into a message.

I've always had this unrelenting desire to produce the written word for people to read and have their lives be changed from the inside out. More importantly, I've learned that the written word is a very powerful tool, and that I've been set apart with certain gifts like writing, which God has prearranged so that he is glorified. When you have a deep passion inside of you, and you crave so badly for others to share this same passion when they do not understand or receive your passion, it can be painful and heartbreaking.

Over the course of my career, I have met some very extraordinary young women who were beaten down because of abuse, abandonment, and rejection, shamed and filled with guilt. These same young women had dreams and ambitions, but somehow through their endless struggle to get others to understand their passion for their dreams, they gave up too soon. Others aren't always going to understand your desires and your dreams. However, this dilemma doesn't stop God from imparting his spirit for his vision into your life.

When your vision is being imparted, what others haven't seen or been a part of is your endless crying out to God, in prayer, worship, listening to your prayers tapes, fasting, and listening to endless worship music. As a result of this, you're trying to block out all of the distraction in your life so that you can hear a fresh revelation from Christ. I do believe that you've not been on your knees in vain. It may feel like it, but not in vain. Being on our knees, crying out to God, it may sometimes feel as though our prayers are being ignored or forgotten, but God hears every word that is being uttered out of your mouth.

Not only does he hear every word that comes out of your mouth, but he knows every thought that you're going to utter before you open your mouth. The most wonderful and splendid thing about God is that before the foundation of this world, he predestined your life. When you tell people that before the world was created, God already knew everything about them, this could possibly overwhelm them. Nevertheless, no matter how overwhelming it may be, God designed your life with love, compassion, and devotion. Not only that, but he positioned your every ability, talent, and gift, so that you could meet your goals, and see your vision come to life.

I love listening to Gospel worship music, and reading God's word, which confirms over and over again how God comes in on time and does the impossible for each of us. There are times when we aren't expecting him to come through, but he proves over and over again that he is an on-time God, looking out for our best interest.

> Read Isaiah 55:8-9. This scripture is the encouragement for this journal entry. "For my thoughts are not your thoughts, Nor are your ways My ways, says the Lord. For as the heavens are higher than your ways, And my thoughts than your thoughts."

**Notes:**

**Notes:**

## Questions for #6:

Whatever it is that you're waiting for God to do in your life, don't give up, because God is going to come through on time.

*When was the last time you felt like giving up?*

*What did you do to keep going?*

*Who were the people who helped you to hang in there?*

*How did they help you?*




*What were the results?*




*How did you feel afterwards?*

**Notes:**

#7

# Out of the Ashes, into His Hands

God's greatness never ceases to amaze me. He demonstrates his love, his mercy, and his grace all day long. Before I decided to write "Out of the Ashes, into His Hands," I was toying with the title, not sure what to name this entry. The day before writing "Out of the Ashes, into His Hands," I was talking to my oldest niece, who lives in San Francisco. She told me good news that God was doing in her life, and that of another niece. She told me that she is to begin working as an eligibility worker for the city and county of San Francisco, and one of her sisters plans to eventually start attending culinary school. After she told me of these things, she then said, "If it wasn't for you, and Big Momma, and Uncle Freddie praying for me, and taking me and my sisters to church, I probably wouldn't have gotten this far."

So what did my oldest niece mean when she made the statement that, "If is wasn't for you, Big Momma and Uncle Freddie," that she probably wouldn't have made it this far? I had an opportunity to later speak with her and she clarified what she meant. She responded with the following statements, "I feel that girls who were abused like I was would benefit from reading this journal." She told me that she would like to tell her own story from her own perspective about her childhood abuse by writing her own book. She further stated that she started this process to write her thoughts down some time ago, but she had to put it down because she felt so emotional about the abuse. I took the time to encourage her that when she is ready to pick up the project again, it would be a good thing, because she feels that girls in her age group would be able to benefit from hearing her perspective. I believe that the message that she and her sisters witnessed actually started with my mother, who not only single-handedly raised five of her own children, but she subsequently raised my nieces.

After I got off the phone with her, it was then that the Holy Spirit spoke to me about the title for this journal entry. When she made those statements, it made me realize that our prayers weren't prayed in vain. Not only were our prayers not prayed in vain, I realized that our prayers, despite the children's upbringing, helped with the covering over their lives.

After our conversation ended, I begin meditating on sermons that I have heard over the years about fruit in my life.

I can honestly say that this was the first time in a very long time that I realized that living a Godly life impacts everyone around you. Now, none of us are perfect, but the simple fact is that the people around us need to see the tangibility of God manifested in our lives. When my nieces watched Christ in our lives, somehow this niece witnessed a message through our mess that God preordained. My mother was not only a superwoman, she was also a forbearer who took a stance against many things in the world that tried to destroy our lives. For most people who knew our mother, they knew a black woman, small in stature, whose demeanor was firm, with a mean hand. However, looking back on her life, she was a person who was firm with perseverance, compassion and love. It was her sole desire to protect and help us survive the dangerous of this world. One way that she protected us was through insisting that we attend church on a regular basis, whether we wanted to or not. Her belief was that we needed to be covered by the blood of Jesus to protect us from the wiles of the enemy.

Not only did she take care of us and her grandchildren, she took care of other people's children. She would take care of other people's children by giving their parents food when they had none. She did this out of compassion and selflessness and her own desire to see these children be cared for. More importantly I witnessed her raise my nieces through shopping for them and bathing them. She helped to keep a shelter over their heads, bought school clothes for them, went to their schools, and attended their graduations. She did many more things for them and us that go beyond the scope of this journal.

As I watched her take care of them, I learned from her that her care for them was a true indication and testament of her love for them. Consequently, watching her live the life of a single mother and grandmother broke my heart, because it simply made me angry, sad, depressed and suicidal.

Yes, you heard me: I was suicidal. There was a time in my life where I felt desperate and angry because we lived in such poverty. Living in poverty simply turned my stomach, because it made me feel that we were different from other people. Somehow, this difference seemed in my mind that others were always more than ten steps ahead of us. At that time in my life when I was a girl, I wanted so desperately not to live in this world because of the pain I had deep inside. I also remember how much I loved my mother, and how awful and horrific it would be if she found me dead in my bedroom.

I remember one day sitting on my bed in a depressed emotional state, and out of that depressed state somehow I desperately cried out to God in prayer to take away the pain I was feeling. Simultaneously, as I prayed to God, he majestically with his awesome power delivered me from the bondage of depression. After that moment in my life, I wasn't perfect, but I knew that I would not return to the bondage of depression.

This is why when I mentioned earlier that when we prayed for my nieces, our prayers weren't in vain, because somehow I knew deep down inside that through God's grace and mercy, he would turn our and their mess into a message.

When you grow close to God, he lets you know through his word the message he has for your life. No matter how bad your situation seems, if God is for you, then who can be against you? If we hear bad news without anything good to combat the bad, we could feel discouraged. I have felt discouragement in my life, especially when I hear about murder and mayhem, about who got gunned down, the stock market crashing, divorce, child abuse, bad schools, broken families, jealousy, family discord, schools closing down, no money for shelter, gas, electricity, food, or clothing. In addition to hearing these "bad things," we also hear that the money isn't there for your teachers to come back for another year, and that your best friends may have to move because their parents lost their home to foreclosure.

When does the madness stop?

When you think that the madness has stopped, there's more bad news. It continues like a massive tsunami. For anyone to listen to bad news constantly could bring on discouragement, desperation, hopelessness, fear, helplessness, depression, anger, and anxiety. Some of these same people who feel these emotions may end up in emergency rooms with panic attacks. Some may enter rehabilitation centers, and some may even file for bankruptcy.

The Bible does tell us about trials and tribulations, but it also tells us about how Jesus Christ has overcome these trials and tribulations we will face in this world. Despite all of the ills in the world, we must not forget that there's God's Good News.

There are scriptures that remind me of God's Good News. Some of it is found in Romans 8:31-32. It reads: "What then shall we say to these things? If God is for us, who can be against us? He who did not spare His own Son, but delivered Him up for us all, how shall He not with Him also freely give us all things?"

This scripture says it all for me, because when I was experiencing a very difficult trial in my life, I meditated on this scripture day and night. It took a while for this trial to end, but it was manageable by meditating on this scripture and not focusing on the trial. I'm not saying that it is easy to not focus on what bothers us, but it is possible. When we look at our situation and feel that these things are against us – and yes, these things in the natural are against us – God says something different. When you feel that the world is against you, then lay it down at the feet of Jesus, and tell those things what the word of God says: If God be for you, then who can be against you?

**Notes:**

**Notes:**

## Questions for #7:

*Who has been against you lately?*




*What do you need to say to these people?*




*Who do you rely on everyday for your strength?*

**Notes:**

#8

# There's No God Like Jehovah.

While reading and writing in this journal, you may have pondered, meditated, and cried as you subsequently poured the word of God over your life. As a result of this transformation, God has joyously stood up with you, and has stood to your attention as you seek his will for your life. This journal had a very long, and profound journey to get into the hands of young women like you. This journal began as a way to reach young women like you, who have struggled with hardship, grief and loss, shame and guilt, abuse, and not having a voice to articulate the depth of your pain and sorrow.

As you read in the dedication page, this journal is a dedication to my mother, whom I must give a standing ovation for the way she lived her life. No, she wasn't a perfect person. However, on a daily basis, she struggled as a woman who had very little in the eyes of the world, but in the eyes of the Lord she was as rich as the richest person in the world. She was rich with grace, mercy, forgiveness, love, friendship, and a legacy that catapulted my life to become a therapist.

What I saw in her life was determination, consistency, a 'do not give up' spirit, dedication, loyalty, commitment, justice, generosity, and honor, as she protected her family from the wiles of the devil, who tried to devour our lives. She was a small woman in stature, but she carried a very big spiritual stick. There are many women like my mother who live in our society, whose voices aren't taken seriously because of either their background, where they grew up, their cultural affiliation, a lack of education or their economic status.

I guarantee you that there are women in your life who don't feel appreciated for the hard work that they've contributed to their families and their communities. Even though their stories are true, it doesn't mean that the Lord cannot come in and change their, and your, circumstances.

As you move through your life, it is very easy to get overwhelmed by your own circumstances. It is easy to give up and give in to the emotional turmoil of your mind, and feel completely defeated by the enemy. I'm a witness with my own experiences, where I wanted to give up, throw in the towel, and say forget it. However, when I felt like giving up and walking away from God, each time the Holy Spirit would whisper very quietly to me, "Do you remember what God has done in your life?"

The Holy Spirit reminded me of the numerous times that God rescued me from circumstances where it felt like an eternity before release came. At the same time that God was speaking to me, the enemy would also try to whisper negative things in my head. He would try to make me believe that God had forsaken and forgotten me. Even as I was writing and creating this journal, my faith was challenged more times than I could count, like the pebbles on the beach.

As you go through life as a young woman, your faith will be challenged more than you can count. However, as your faith is being challenged, you might want to give up and maybe throw in the towel. When you feel this way, this is when we become vulnerable to the negative messages from others and the depraved messages from enemy.

The first entry in this journal began the process that told the story about how our God is very excited about you, and the purpose he has for your life. At this time, you're probably still wondering the same questions from when we began this journey:

"Where do I fit in with the Body of Christ?"
"Where do I fit in with my family, my church, my school, and my community?"

There's a scripture that could answer some of your questions, found in Jeremiah 29:11. God is speaking to you by saying, "The thoughts that I have toward you are thoughts of peace, and not of evil, to give you a future, and a hope."

At this moment, you might feel alone, you might feel betrayed, forgotten, or misunderstood. No matter how you feel, these feelings do not dictate your path. I've LEARNED throughout my own life that it takes time to meditate on the word of God, to be patient with God while going through a cyclone of rough waters in you life.

Lastly, do not be afraid to ask God questions about the path and direction that he has for your life, for he is no respecter of persons.

Well, girls, my time is up. I pray that each of you, from the bottom of your hearts, have enjoyed this journey. I know that I have.

**Notes:**

**Notes:**

## Questions on #8:

*Where am I on the patience scale, waiting on God? (low, medium, high, really impatient)*

*What do I need to do today to change how I feel?*

*What would be helpful or not helpful?*

**God isn't done with you yet, because he knows greatness when he sees it.**

**Notes:**

www.ingramcontent.com/pod-product-compliance
Lightning Source LLC
LaVergne TN
LVHW091406290126
830673LV00013B/640